Life Lessons
from THE INSPIRED WORD of GOD

BOOK of
1 CORINTHIANS

MAX LUCADO
General Editor

TABLE OF CONTENTS

HOW TO STUDY THE BIBLE

BY MAX LUCADO

*T*his is a peculiar book you are holding. Words crafted in another language. Deeds done in a distant era. Events recorded in a far-off land. Counsel offered to a foreign people. This is a peculiar book.

It's surprising that anyone reads it. It's too old. Some of its writings date back five thousand years. It's too bizarre. The book speaks of incredible floods, fires, earthquakes, and people with supernatural abilities. It's too radical. The Bible calls for undying devotion to a carpenter who called himself God's Son.

Logic says this book shouldn't survive. Too old, too bizarre, too radical.

The Bible has been banned, burned, scoffed, and ridiculed. Scholars have mocked it as foolish. Kings have branded it as illegal. A thousand times over it the grave has been dug and the dirge has begun, but somehow the Bible never stays in the grave. Not only has it survived, it has thrived. It is the single most popular book in all of history. It has been the best-selling book in the world for years!

There is no way on earth to explain it. Which perhaps is the only explanation. The answer? The Bible's durability is not found on earth; it is found in heaven. For the millions who have tested its claims and claimed its promises, there is but one answer—the Bible is God's book and God's voice.

As you read it, you would be wise to give some thought to two questions. What is the purpose of the Bible? and How do I study the Bible? Time spent reflecting on these two issues will greatly enhance your Bible study.

What is the purpose of the Bible?

Let the Bible itself answer that question.

Since you were a child you have known the Holy Scriptures which are able to make you wise. And that wisdom leads to salvation through faith in Christ Jesus.

(2 Tim. 3:15)

The purpose of the Bible? Salvation. God's highest passion is to get his children home. His book, the Bible, describes his plan of salvation. The purpose of the Bible is to proclaim God's plan and passion to save his children.

That is the reason this book has endured through the centuries. It dares to tackle the toughest questions about life: Where do I go after I die? Is there a God? What do I do with my fears? The Bible offers answers to these crucial questions. It is the treasure map that leads us to God's highest treasure, eternal life.

But how do we use the Bible? Countless copies of Scripture sit unread on bookshelves and nightstands simply because people don't know how to read it. What can we do to make the Bible real in our lives?

The clearest answer is found in the words of Jesus.

"Ask," he promised, *"and God will give it to you. Search and you will find. Knock, and the door will open for you."*

(Matt. 7:7)

The first step in understanding the Bible is asking God to help us. We should read prayerfully. If anyone understands God's Word, it is because of God and not the reader.

But the Helper will teach you everything and will cause you to remember all that I told you. The Helper is the Holy Spirit whom the Father will send in my name.

(John 14:24)

Before reading the Bible, pray. Invite God to speak to you. Don't go to Scripture looking for your idea, go searching for his.

Not only should we read the Bible prayerfully, we should read it carefully. *Search and you will find* is the pledge. The Bible is not a newspaper to be skimmed but rather a mine to be quarried. *Search for it like silver, and hunt for it like hidden treasure. Then you will understand respect for the LORD, and you will find that you know God* (Prov. 2:4).

Any worthy find requires effort. The Bible is no exception. To understand the Bible you don't have to be brilliant, but you must be willing to roll up your sleeves and search.

Be a worker who is not ashamed and who uses the true teaching in the right way.

(2 Tim. 2:15)

Here's a practical point. Study the Bible a bit at a time. Hunger is not satisfied by eating twenty-one meals in one sitting once a week. The body needs a steady diet to remain strong. So does the soul. When God sent food to his people in the wilderness, he didn't provide loaves already made. Instead, he sent them manna in the shape of *thin flakes, like frost . . . on the desert ground* (Exod. 16:14).

God gave manna in limited portions.

God sends spiritual food the same way. He opens the heavens with just enough nutrients for today's hunger. He provides, *a command here, a command there. A rule here, a rule there. A little lesson here, a little lesson there* (Isa. 28:10).

Don't be discouraged if your reading reaps a small harvest. Some days a lesser portion is all that is needed. What is important is to search every day for that day's message. A steady diet of God's Word over a lifetime builds a healthy soul and mind.

A little girl returned from her first day at school. Her mom asked, "Did you learn anything?" "Apparently not enough," the girl responded. "I have to go back tomorrow and the next day and the next. . . ."

Such is the case with learning. And such is the case with Bible study. Understanding comes little by little over a lifetime.

There is a third step in understanding the Bible. After the asking and seeking comes the knocking. *After* you ask and search, then knock.

Knock, and the door will open for you.
(Matt. 7:7)

To knock is to stand at God's door. To make yourself available. To climb the steps, cross the porch, stand at the doorway, and volunteer. Knocking goes beyond the realm of thinking and into the realm of acting.

To knock is to ask, What can I do? How can I obey? Where can I go?

It's one thing to know what to do. It's another to do it. But for those who do it, those who choose to obey, a special reward awaits them.

The truly happy are those who carefully study God's perfect law that makes people free, and they continue to study it. They do not forget what they heard, but they obey what God's teaching says. Those who do this will be made happy.
(James 1:25)

What a promise. Happiness comes to those who do what they read! It's the same with medicine. If you only read the label but ignore the pills, it won't help. It's the same with food. If you only read the recipe but never cook, you won't be fed. And it's the same with the Bible. If you only read the words but never obey, you'll never know the joy God has promised.

Ask. Search. Knock. Simple, isn't it? Why don't you give it a try? If you do, you'll see why you are holding the most remarkable book in history.

INTRODUCTION

*A*n Indian was walking up a mountain when he heard a voice.

"Carry me with you," it requested.

The Indian turned and saw a snake. He refused. "If I carry you up the mountain you will bite me."

"I wouldn't do that," the snake assured. "All I need is some help. I am slow and you are fast; please be kind and carry me to the top of the mountain."

It was against his better judgment, but the Indian agreed. He picked up the snake, put him in his shirt, and resumed the journey. When they reached the top, he reached in his shirt to remove the snake and got bit.

He fell to the ground, and the snake slithered away.

"You lied!" the Indian cried. "You said you wouldn't bite me."

The snake stopped and looked back, "I didn't lie. You knew who I was when you picked me up."

We hear the legend and shake our heads. He should have known better, we bemoan. And we are right. He should have. And so should we. But don't we do the same? Don't we believe the lies of the snake? Don't we pick up what we should leave alone?

The Corinthian Christians did. One snake after another had hissed lies in their ears, and they had believed it. How many lies did they believe?

How much time do you have?

The list is long and ugly: sectarianism, disunity, sexual immorality. And that is only the first six chapters.

But First Corinthians is more than a list of sins, it is an epistle of patience. Paul initiates the letter by calling these Christians "brothers." He could have called them heretics or hypocrites or skirt-chasers (and in so many words he does), but not before he calls them brothers.

He patiently teaches them about worship, unity, the role of women, and the Lord's Supper. He writes as if he can see them face to face. He is disturbed but not despondent. Angry but not desperate. His driving passion is love. And his treatise on love in chapter 13 remains the greatest essay ever penned.

The letter, however personal, is not just for Corinth. It is for all who have heard the whisper and felt the fangs. We, like the Indian, should have known better. We, like the Corinthians, sometimes need a second chance.

LESSON ONE

THE FOOLISHNESS OF HUMAN WISDOM

REFLECTION

Begin your study by sharing thoughts on this question.

1. Which aspects of the gospel (Jesus' life, death, and resurrection) are difficult for people to understand and accept?

_____

_____

_____

BIBLE READING

Read 1 Corinthians 1:18–31 from the NCV or the NKJV.

NCV

¹⁸The teaching about the cross is foolishness to those who are being lost, but to us who are being saved it is the power of God. ¹⁹It is written in the Scriptures:
"I will cause the wise men to lose their
  wisdom;
  I will make the wise men unable to
  understand."
²⁰Where is the wise person? Where is the educated person? Where is the skilled talker of this world? God has made the wisdom of the

NKJV

¹⁸For the message of the cross is foolishness to those who are perishing, but to us who are being saved it is the power of God. ¹⁹For it is written:

"I will destroy the wisdom of the wise,
  And bring to nothing the understanding of
  the prudent."

²⁰Where *is* the wise? Where *is* the scribe? Where *is* the disputer of this age? Has not God

NCV

world foolish. ²¹In the wisdom of God the world did not know God through its own wisdom. So God chose to use the message that sounds foolish to save those who believe. ²²The Jews ask for miracles, and the Greeks want wisdom. ²³But we preach a crucified Christ. This is a big problem to the Jews, and it is foolishness to those who are not Jews. ²⁴But Christ is the power of God and the wisdom of God to those people God has called—Jews and Greeks. ²⁵Even the foolishness of God is wiser than human wisdom, and the weakness of God is stronger than human strength.

²⁶Brothers and sisters, look at what you were when God called you. Not many of you were wise in the way the world judges wisdom. Not many of you had great influence. Not many of you came from important families. ²⁷But God chose the foolish things of the world to shame the wise, and he chose the weak things of the world to shame the strong. ²⁸He chose what the world thinks is unimportant and what the world looks down on and thinks is nothing in order to destroy what the world thinks is important. ²⁹God did this so that no one can brag in his presence. ³⁰Because of God you are in Christ Jesus, who has become for us wisdom from God. In Christ we are put right with God, and have been made holy, and have been set free from sin. ³¹So, as the Scripture says, "If someone wants to brag, he should brag only about the Lord."

NKJV

made foolish the wisdom of this world? ²¹For since, in the wisdom of God, the world through wisdom did not know God, it pleased God through the foolishness of the message preached to save those who believe. ²²For Jews request a sign, and Greeks seek after wisdom; ²³but we preach Christ crucified, to the Jews a stumbling block and to the Greeks foolishness, ²⁴but to those who are called, both Jews and Greeks, Christ the power of God and the wisdom of God. ²⁵Because the foolishness of God is wiser than men, and the weakness of God is stronger than men.

²⁶For you see your calling, brethren, that not many wise according to the flesh, not many mighty, not many noble, *are called*. ²⁷But God has chosen the foolish things of the world to put to shame the wise, and God has chosen the weak things of the world to put to shame the things which are mighty; ²⁸and the base things of the world and the things which are despised God has chosen, and the things which are not, to bring to nothing the things that are, ²⁹that no flesh should glory in His presence. ³⁰But of Him you are in Christ Jesus, who became for us wisdom from God—and righteousness and sanctification and redemption— ³¹that, as it is written, "He who glories, let him glory in the LORD."

DISCOVERY

Explore the Bible reading by discussing these questions.

2. In what ways can the gospel seem foolish?

_____

_____

_____

3. How do Jesus' life and death reveal the wisdom and power of God?

_____

_____

_____

4. In what ways is God's wisdom different from the world's wisdom?

_____

_____

_____

5. What does Paul mean when he says God "chose the weak things of the world"?

_____

_____

_____

6. So, what do believers have to brag about?

_____

_____

_____

INSPIRATION

Here is an uplifting thought from *The Inspirational Bible*.

You want success? Here's your model. You want achievement? Here's your prototype. You want bright lights, pageants, and media attention? Consider the front-page, center article of the nation's largest daily newspaper.

It is a caricature of "Miss America." The vital data of the fifty-one participants has been compiled to present the perfect woman. She has brown hair. She has brown eyes. She knows how to sing and has a perfect figure: 35-24-35. She is Miss America.

The message trumpets off the page: "This is the standard for American women." The implication is clear: Do what it takes to be like her. Firm your thighs. Deepen your cleavage. Pamper your hair. Improve your walk.

No reference is made to her convictions . . . to her honesty . . . to her faith . . . or to her God. But you are told her hip size.

In a small photo, four inches to the left, is another woman. Her face is thin. Her skin is wrinkled, almost leathery. No makeup . . . no blush . . . no lipstick. There is a faint smile on her lips and a glint in her eyes. She looks pale. Perhaps it's my imagination or perhaps it's

time. The caption read, "Mother Teresa: In serious condition."

Mother Teresa. You know her story. When she won the Nobel Peace Prize in 1985, she gave the two hundred thousand dollars to the poor of Calcutta. When a businessman bought her a new car, she sold it and gave the money to the underprivileged. She owns nothing. She owes nothing.

Two women: Miss America and Mother Teresa. One walks the boardwalk; the other walks the alley. Two voices. One promises crowns, flowers, and crowds. The other promises service, surrender, and joy.

Now I have nothing against beauty pageants (although I have my reservations about them). But I do have something against the lying voices that noise our world.

You've heard them. They tell you to swap your integrity for a new sale. To barter your convictions for an easy deal. To exchange your devotion for a quick thrill.

They whisper. They woo. They taunt. They tantalize. They flirt. They flatter. "Go ahead, it's O.K." "Just wait until tomorrow." "Don't worry,

no one will know." "How could anything that feels so right be so wrong?" . . .

For amidst the fleeting promises of pleasure is the timeless promise of [God's] presence.

"Surely I am with you always, to the very end of the age."

"Never will I leave you; never will I forsake you."

There is no chorus so loud that the voice of God cannot be heard . . . if we will but listen.

(From *In the Eye of the Storm* by Max Lucado)

RESPONSE

Use these questions to share more deeply with each other.

7. In what ways does the media entice us to accept the world's values?

---

8. Have you sought God's guidance, rather than relying on your own intellect and ability? Explain the circumstances and the outcome.

---

9. In what ways can we ignore the false messages around us and think more like God?

_____

_____

_____

PRAYER

Father, too often the lies of the world drown out your voice. Give us ears to hear you and hearts willing to obey. Help us to stand against the pressure to seek success and power. Give us the strength to choose the timeless truths of your Word over the fleeting promises of the world. And Father, confirm only those thoughts and plans that conform to your will.

JOURNALING

Take a few moments to record your personal insights from this lesson.

In light of this passage, how can I make better decisions?

18

ADDITIONAL QUESTIONS

10. Why is it important to recognize the limits of human wisdom?

_____

_____

_____

11. In what ways can you determine if an idea or plan is based on worldly thinking or biblical teaching?

_____

_____

_____

12. List some benefits of living according to God's wisdom instead of human wisdom.

_____

_____

_____

For more Bible passages on the limits of human wisdom, see Proverbs 3:5, 7; Ecclesiastes 1:12–18; 2:16; Jeremiah 9:23–24; Ezekiel 28:2–7; Matthew 11:25; 1 Corinthians 3:19,20.

To complete the book of 1 Corinthians during this twelve-part study, read 1 Corinthians 1:1–31.

LESSON TWO

GOD'S WISDOM REVEALED

REFLECTION

Begin your study by sharing thoughts on this question.

1. Think of someone who consistently gives you good advice. Specifically, how has that person's wise counsel helped you?

_____

_____

_____

BIBLE READING

Read 1 Corinthians 2:6–16 from the NCV or the NKJV.

NCV

⁶However, I speak a wisdom to those who are mature. But this wisdom is not from this world or from the rulers of this world, who are losing their power. ⁷I speak God's secret wisdom, which he has kept hidden. Before the world began, God planned this wisdom for our glory. ⁸None of the rulers of this world understood it. If they had, they would not have crucified the Lord of glory. ⁹But as it is written in the Scriptures:

NKJV

⁶However, we speak wisdom among those who are mature, yet not the wisdom of this age, nor of the rulers of this age, who are coming to nothing. ⁷But we speak the wisdom of God in a mystery, the hidden *wisdom* which God ordained before the ages for our glory, ⁸which none of the rulers of this age knew; for had they known, they would not have crucified the Lord of glory.

⁹But as it is written:

NCV

"No one has ever seen this,
  and no one has ever heard about it.
No one has ever imagined
  what God has prepared for those
  who love him."

[10]But God has shown us these things through the Spirit.

The Spirit searches out all things, even the deep secrets of God. [11]Who knows the thoughts that another person has? Only a person's spirit that lives within him knows his thoughts. It is the same with God. No one knows the thoughts of God except the Spirit of God. [12]Now we did not receive the spirit of the world, but we received the Spirit that is from God so that we can know all that God has given us. [13]And we speak about these things, not with words taught us by human wisdom but with words taught us by the Spirit. And so we explain spiritual truths to spiritual people. [14]A person who does not have the Spirit does not accept the truths that come from the Spirit of God. That person thinks they are foolish and cannot understand them, because they can only be judged to be true by the Spirit. [15]The spiritual person is able to judge all things, but no one can judge him. The Scripture says:

[16]"Who has known the mind of the Lord?
  Who has been able to teach him?"
But we have the mind of Christ.

NKJV

"Eye has not seen, nor ear heard,
Nor have entered into the heart of man
The things which God has prepared for
  those who love Him."

[10]But God has revealed *them* to us through His Spirit. For the Spirit searches all things, yes, the deep things of God. [11]For what man knows the things of a man except the spirit of the man which is in him? Even so no one knows the things of God except the Spirit of God. [12]Now we have received, not the spirit of the world, but the Spirit who is from God, that we might know the things that have been freely given to us by God.

[13]These things we also speak, not in words which man's wisdom teaches but which the Holy Spirit teaches, comparing spiritual things with spiritual. [14]But the natural man does not receive the things of the Spirit of God, for they are foolishness to him; nor can he know *them*, because they are spiritually discerned. [15]But he who is spiritual judges all things, yet he himself is *rightly* judged by no one. [16]For "who has known the mind of the LORD that he may instruct Him?" But we have the mind of Christ.

DISCOVERY

Explore the Bible reading by discussing these questions.

2. Why does God keep some things hidden from us?

_____

_____

_____

3. In what ways can we know God's thoughts and plans?

_____

_____

_____

4. List some ways the Holy Spirit helps believers.

_____

_____

_____

5. Why is a person without the Spirit unable to understand spiritual truths?

_____

_____

_____

6. Explain what it means to "have the mind of Christ."

_____

_____

_____

INSPIRATION

Here is an uplifting thought from *The Inspirational Bible*.

Men are always seeking for greater wisdom, but they usually bypass the Ultimate Source of wisdom. The Scriptures clearly point this direction. They reveal, "The fear of the Lord is the beginning of wisdom, and the knowledge of the Holy One is understanding" (Proverbs 9:10). But what has man done with this tremendous resource at his fingertips? Ignored it! "For even though they knew God, they did not honor Him as God, or give thanks; but they became futile in their speculations, and their foolish heart was darkened. Professing to be wise, they became fools" (Romans 1:21,22).

Since God's wisdom resides in His Word, it is imperative to know what He has revealed, but even many Christians ignore a regular time of reading and studying the Scriptures. Therefore, many of their decisions are foolish, because they've not consulted the Ultimate Source of wisdom.

(From *Finding Time*
by Rick Yohn)

RESPONSE

Use these questions to share more deeply with each other.

7.   In what different ways do we try to gain wisdom?

_____

_____

_____

8.   What happens when we rely on human wisdom, instead of God's wisdom?

_____

_____

_____

9.   When has the Holy Spirit helped you understand or apply God's Word?

_____

_____

_____

PRAYER

Father, your plans for us are perfect. Yet we often doubt your promises, assuming we can take better care of ourselves than our Creator. Forgive us for ignoring the truth in your Word. Tune our ears to your Spirit's voice, and teach us to follow your ways. May our lives testify to your great wisdom and power.

JOURNALING

Take a few moments to record your personal insights from this lesson.

How can I weed out the "thorns" that hinder my spiritual growth?

ADDITIONAL QUESTIONS

10. What practical steps can we take to reduce the risk of making foolish decisions?

_____

_____

_____

11. What sometimes keeps you from seeking God's help?

_____

_____

_____

12. In what ways can you depend more on God's Spirit to help you make wise decisions?

_____

_____

_____

For more Bible passages on God's wisdom, see Psalm 111:10; Proverbs 2:6; Isaiah 11:2; Jeremiah 10:12; Ephesians 1:16,17; Colossians 2:3; 2 Timothy 3:15; James 1:5.

To complete the book of 1 Corinthians during this twelve-part study, read 1 Corinthians 2:1–3:8.

ADDITIONAL THOUGHTS

LESSON THREE

WORK THAT LASTS

REFLECTION

Begin your study by sharing thoughts on this question.

1. What usually motivates people to volunteer in the community or church?

_____

_____

_____

BIBLE READING

Read 1 Corinthians 3:9–15 from the NCV or the NKJV.

NCV

⁹We are God's workers, working together; you are like God's farm, God's house.

¹⁰Using the gift God gave me, I laid the foundation of that house like an expert builder. Others are building on that foundation, but all people should be careful how they build on it. ¹¹The foundation that has already been laid is Jesus Christ, and no one can lay down any other foundation. ¹²But if people build on that foundation, using gold, silver, jewels, wood, grass, or straw, ¹³their work will be clearly seen, because the Day of Judgment will make it

NKJV

⁹For we are God's fellow workers; you are God's field, *you are* God's building. ¹⁰According to the grace of God which was given to me, as a wise master builder I have laid the foundation, and another builds on it. But let each one take heed how he builds on it. ¹¹For no other foundation can anyone lay than that which is laid, which is Jesus Christ. ¹²Now if anyone builds on this foundation *with* gold, silver, precious stones, wood, hay, straw, ¹³each one's work will become clear; for the Day will declare it, because it will be revealed by fire; and the fire

NCV

visible. That Day will appear with fire, and the fire will test everyone's work to show what sort of work it was. [14]If the building that has been put on the foundation still stands, the builder will get a reward. [15]But if the building is burned up, the builder will suffer loss. The builder will be saved, but it will be as one who escaped from a fire.

NKJV

will test each one's work, of what sort it is. [14]If anyone's work which he has built on *it* endures, he will receive a reward. [15]If anyone's work is burned, he will suffer loss; but he himself will be saved, yet so as through fire.

DISCOVERY

Explore the Bible reading by discussing these questions.

2. Jesus is the foundation of the church. What does that mean in today's world?

_____

_____

_____

3. In what ways can we build on the foundation that God has laid?

_____

_____

_____

4. God will test the quality of our work like fire tests the quality of building materials. What kinds of work will withstand that test?

_____

_____

_____

5. What are the rewards of building God's kingdom faithfully and with the best materials?

_____

_____

_____

6. Work for God that is less than excellent is compared to a straw house that will burn up in the fire of judgment. What kind of behavior or service is like a straw house?

_____

_____

_____

INSPIRATION

Here is an uplifting thought from *The Inspirational Bible*.

From the looks of things, you're pretty impressive. You've got a nice place. And I suppose your neighbors would agree that you're a hard worker . . . climbing right on up that ladder toward success, right? I realize you're not into big bucks; but face it, nobody's going hungry. Far from it. Your job is fairly secure. Making more money than ever, you're on your way. But wait, I want to know about the "other half." These things I've mentioned are all external—physical and material stuff. What I want to know is how things are internally.

You look secure and successful, but the half has not been told, right? Part of you is insecure and fearful. Underneath, you're pretty weak. You appear to be happy, easy-going, and fulfilled; but the half has not been told, has it? You wonder about where all this is leading you. Your restless drive for more and your desire for calm, peaceful contentment seem poles apart . . . because they are poles apart. Deep down, nothing within you smiles.

Your salary is good and your material possessions are growing in number, but again, the half has not been told. The truth is that you are empty on the inside and you're faking it on the outside. Not one thing you own in all your "kingdom" has brought you the happiness you long for. So you're thinking, "Maybe if I could land that better job," or "get into that bigger house," or . . . or . . .

But don't allow the smoke screen of more money to blind your eyes to the truth. There's a lot more to being rich than making more money. Seneca, the Roman, was right, "Money has never yet made anyone rich." Do you want riches? Then listen to Jesus: "But seek first His kingdom and His righteousness, and all these things shall be added to you."

For the real riches, try switching kingdoms.

(From *Living on the Ragged Edge*
by Charles Swindoll)

RESPONSE

Use these questions to share more deeply with each other.

7. What should be the driving force behind our work for God?

_____

_____

_____

8. Why is it tempting to evaluate our success according to external results?

_____

_____

_____

9. Describe what kind of work counts for eternity.

_____

_____

_____

PRAYER

Father, thank you for laying the perfect foundation for your church. Now show us how to build on that foundation. Give us a burning desire to build your church. Help us to see what is important and what is lasting. Let us make decisions based on eternity and not on temporary possessions. Most of all, Father, help us to seek your Kingdom and your righteousness.

JOURNALING

Take a few moments to record your personal insights from this lesson.

What is my role in building God's church?

ADDITIONAL QUESTIONS

10. What obstacles keep us from getting more involved in ministry?

_____

_____

_____

11. In what ways can we evaluate the quality of our service?

_____

_____

_____

12. List some practical ways you can invest yourself in God's kingdom.

_____

_____

_____

For more Bible passages on work that lasts, see Luke 12:33; John 6:27; 2 Corinthians 4:17,18; Colossians 3:23,24; Hebrews 10:34,35.

To complete the book of 1 Corinthians during this twelve–part study, read 1 Corinthians 3:9–23.

ADDITIONAL THOUGHTS

LESSON FOUR

SERVING CHRIST

REFLECTION

Begin your study by sharing thoughts on this question.

1. Think of someone who has served Christ for many years. In what ways has that person's example inspired you?

_____

_____

_____

BIBLE READING

Read 1 Corinthians 4:6–19 from the NCV or the NKJV.

NCV

⁶Brothers and sisters, I have used Apollos and myself as examples so you could learn through us the meaning of the saying, "Follow only what is written in the Scriptures." Then you will not be more proud of one person than another. ⁷Who says you are better than others? What do you have that was not given to you? And if it was given to you, why do you brag as if you did not receive it as a gift?

⁸You think you already have everything you need. You think you are rich. You think you have

NKJV

⁶Now these things, brethren, I have figuratively transferred to myself and Apollos for your sakes, that you may learn in us not to think beyond what is written, that none of you may be puffed up on behalf of one against the other. ⁷For who makes you differ _from another?_ And what do you have that you did not receive? Now if you did indeed receive _it,_ why do you boast as if you had not received _it?_

⁸You are already full! You are already rich! You have reigned as kings without us—and

become kings without us. I wish you really were kings so we could be kings together with you. [9]But it seems to me that God has put us apostles in last place, like those sentenced to die. We are like a show for the whole world to see—angels and people. [10]We are fools for Christ's sake, but you are very wise in Christ. We are weak, but you are strong. You receive honor, but we are shamed. [11]Even to this very hour we do not have enough to eat or drink or to wear. We are often beaten, and we have no homes in which to live. [12]We work hard with our own hands for our food. When people curse us, we bless them. When they hurt us, we put up with it. [13]When they tell evil lies about us, we speak nice words about them. Even today, we are treated as though we were the garbage of the world—the filth of the earth.

[14]I am not trying to make you feel ashamed. I am writing this to give you a warning as my own dear children. [15]For though you may have ten thousand teachers in Christ, you do not have many fathers. Through the Good News I became your father in Christ Jesus, [16]so I beg you, please follow my example. [17]That is why I am sending to you Timothy, my son in the Lord. I love Timothy, and he is faithful. He will help you remember my way of life in Christ Jesus, just as I teach it in all the churches everywhere.

[18]Some of you have become proud, thinking that I will not come to you again. [19]But I will come to you very soon if the Lord wishes. Then I will know what the proud ones do, not what they say, . . .

indeed I could wish you did reign, that we also might reign with you! [9]For I think that God has displayed us, the apostles, last, as men condemned to death; for we have been made a spectacle to the world, both to angels and to men. [10]We *are* fools for Christ's sake, but you *are* wise in Christ! We *are* weak, but you *are* strong! You *are* distinguished, but we *are* dishonored! [11]To the present hour we both hunger and thirst, and we are poorly clothed, and beaten, and homeless. [12]And we labor, working with our own hands. Being reviled, we bless; being persecuted, we endure; [13]being defamed, we entreat. We have been made as the filth of the world, the offscouring of all things until now.

[14]I do not write these things to shame you, but as my beloved children I warn *you*. [15]For though you might have ten thousand instructors in Christ, yet *you do* not *have* many fathers; for in Christ Jesus I have begotten you through the gospel. [16]Therefore I urge you, imitate me. [17]For this reason I have sent Timothy to you, who is my beloved and faithful son in the Lord, who will remind you of my ways in Christ, as I teach everywhere in every church.

[18]Now some are puffed up, as though I were not coming to you. [19]But I will come to you shortly, if the Lord wills, and I will know, not the word of those who are puffed up, but the power.

DISCOVERY

Explore the Bible reading by discussing these questions.

2. Paul saw evidence of spiritual pride in the early church. Why did that trouble him?

_____

_____

_____

3. Our abilities and talents are gifts from God. How should knowing that keep us from thinking that we are better than others?

_____

_____

_____

4. Is there anything wrong with taking the credit for our accomplishments?

_____

_____

_____

5. Paul believed apostles should stand in last place. What does that tell us about Paul's attitude toward status and position?

_____

_____

_____

6. What should we be willing to give up to serve Christ?

_____

_____

_____

INSPIRATION

Here is an uplifting thought from *The Inspirational Bible.*

The scene is almost spooky: a tall, unfinished tower looming solitarily on a dusty plain. Its base is wide and strong but covered with weeds. Large stones originally intended for use in the tower lie forsaken on the ground. Buckets, hammers, and pulleys—all lie abandoned. The silhouette cast by the structure is lean and lonely.

Not too long ago, this tower was buzzing with activity. A bystander would have been impressed with the smooth-running construction of the world's first skyscraper. One group of workers stirred freshly made mortar. Another team pulled bricks out of the oven. A third group carried the bricks to the construction site while a fourth shouldered the load up a winding path to the top of the tower where it was firmly set in place.

Their dream was a tower. A tower that would be taller than anyone had ever dreamed. A tower that would punch through the clouds and scratch the heavens. And what was the purpose of the tower? To glorify God? No. To try to find God? No. To call people to look upward to God? Try again. To provide a heavenly haven of prayer? Still wrong.

The purpose of the work caused its eventual abortion. The method was right. The plan was effective. But the motive was wrong. Dead wrong. Read these minutes from the "Tower Planning Committee Meeting" and see what I mean:

"Come, let us build ourselves a city, and a tower with its top in the heavens, and [watch out] let us make a name for ourselves."

Why was the tower being built? Selfishness. Pure, 100 percent selfishness. The bricks were made of inflated egos and the mortar was made of pride. Men were giving sweat and blood for a pillar. Why? So that somebody's name could be remembered.

We have a name for that: blind ambition.

We make heroes out of people who are ambitious.

And rightly so. This world would be in sad shape without people who dream of touching the heavens. Ambition is that grit in the soul which creates disenchantment with the ordinary and puts the dare into dreams.

But left unchecked it becomes an insatiable addition to power and prestige; a roaring hunger for achievement that devours people as a lion devours an animal, leaving behind only the skeletal remains of relationships.

Blind ambition. Distorted values.

God won't tolerate it. He didn't then and he won't now. He took the "Climb to Heaven Campaign" into his hands. With one sweep he painted the tower gray with confusion and sent workers babbling in all directions. He took man's greatest achievement and blew it into the winds like a child blows a dandelion.

Are you building any towers? Examine your motives. And remember the statement imprinted on the base of the windswept Tower of Babel: Blind ambition is a giant step away from God and one step closer to catastrophe.

(From *God Came Near* by Max Lucado)

RESPONSE

Use these questions to share more deeply with each other.

7. What is the potential danger in trying to achieve great things for God?

_____

_____

_____

8. What are some ways selfish ambition can create problems in the church?

_____

_____

_____

9. How can we determine whether our service to God is Christ-centered or self-centered?

_____

_____

_____

PRAYER

O Father, forgive us for our arrogance; for acting as though we can accomplish great things on our own. We are nothing without you. Teach us to recognize our complete dependence on you and to surrender our desires and ambitions. Make our service more pleasing in your sight.

JOURNALING

Take a few moments to record your personal insights from this lesson.

What personal goals or desires do I need to reevaluate, in light of this passage?

ADDITIONAL QUESTIONS

10. In what ways can we curb our appetite for prestige and power?

_____

_____

_____

11. When God gives us success in ministry, how can we guard against pride?

_____

_____

_____

12. How can we give God credit for the things he has accomplished through us?

_____

_____

_____

For more Bible passages on serving Christ, see Matthew 20:25–28; John 12:25,26; Romans 12:10,11; 14:17,18; Ephesians 6:7.

To complete the book of 1 Corinthians during this twelve–part study, read 1 Corinthians 4:1–6:20.

LESSON FIVE

SELF-SACRIFICE

REFLECTION

Begin your study by sharing thoughts on this question.

1. Describe a time when someone sacrificed his or her own needs to help you.

_____

_____

_____

BIBLE READING

Read 1 Corinthians 9:16–22 from the NCV or the NKJV.

NCV

[16]Telling the Good News does not give me any reason for bragging. Telling the Good News is my duty—something I must do. And how terrible it will be for me if I do not tell the Good News. [17]If I preach because it is my own choice, I have a reward. But if I preach and it is not my choice to do so, I am only doing the duty that was given to me. [18]So what reward do I get? This is my reward: that when I tell the Good News I can offer it freely. I do not use my full rights in my work of preaching the Good News.

[19]I am free and belong to no one. But I make

NKJV

[16]For if I preach the gospel, I have nothing to boast of, for necessity is laid upon me; yes, woe is me if I do not preach the gospel! [17]For if I do this willingly, I have a reward; but if against my will, I have been entrusted with a stewardship. [18]What is my reward then? That when I preach the gospel, I may present the gospel of Christ without charge, that I may not abuse my authority in the gospel.

[19]For though I am free from all *men*, I have made myself a servant to all, that I might win the more; [20]and to the Jews I became as a Jew,

NCV

myself a slave to all people to win as many as I can. ²⁰To the Jews I became like a Jew to win the Jews. I myself am not ruled by the law. But to those who are ruled by the law I became like a person who is ruled by the law. I did this to win those who are ruled by the law. ²¹To those who are without the law I became like a person who is without the law. I did this to win those people who are without the law. (But really, I am not without God's law—I am ruled by Christ's law.) ²²To those who are weak, I became weak so I could win the weak. I have become all things to all people so I could save some of them in any way possible.

NKJV

that I might win Jews; to those *who are* under the law, as under the law, that I might win those *who are* under the law; ²¹to those *who are* without law, as without law (not being without law toward God, but under law toward Christ), that I might win those *who are* without law; ²²to the weak I became as weak, that I might win the weak. I have become all things to all *men,* that I might by all means save some.

DISCOVERY

Explore the Bible reading by discussing these questions.

2. Paul gave up some of his rights to preach the Good News. Why did he do that?

_____

_____

_____

3. Explain what it means to become a "slave to all people."

_____

_____

_____

4. Paul was not as concerned with his method of evangelism as with the message he was proclaiming. How can we apply his thinking to our evangelism today?

_____

_____

_____

5. Think about the times you try to be a witness for Christ. How can you share your experience with others?

_____

_____

_____

6. What can hinder our Christian witness?

_____

_____

_____

INSPIRATION

Here is an uplifting thought from *The Inspirational Bible*.

In the rough and tumble of our abrasive twentieth century, humility is scarcely considered a virtue. Such qualities as meekness and gentleness are not the sort that most people seek in order to succeed. We are fast moving, masterful, permissive people who from the cradle learn to shove and push and scream and scramble to get ahead—to plant our proud feet on the top of the totem pole.

Fiercely we contend for our rights, believing the strange philosophy that to be big and bold and brazen is best. We subscribe to the idea that since no one else will blow my horn for me, I must blow my own bugle loudly and long. We are completely convinced that unless we make our own mark in the world we will be forgotten in the crush—obliterated from memory by the milling masses around us.

From the hour we begin to take our first feeble, frightened steps as tiny tots we are exhorted to "stand on your own feet." We are urged and encouraged to "make it on your own." We are told to "make your own decisions." We are stimulated to be aggressive, self-assertive, and very self-assured. All of these attributes we are sure will lead to ultimate greatness.

In the face of all this it comes to us as a distinct shock to hear our Lord declare: "whosoever therefore shall humble himself as this little child, the same is greatest in the kingdom of heaven." . . .

The selfless, self-effacing character of God's love simply does not permit it to strut and parade itself pompously. It will have no part of such a performance. It is not proud, arrogant, puffed up with its own importance.

(From *A Gardener Looks at the Fruits of the Spirit* by Philip Keller)

RESPONSE

Use these questions to share more deeply with each other.

7. In this lesson's Bible passage Paul said he gave up his own rights, preferences, and styles in order to share the gospel. How does this contradict human nature?

_____

_____

_____

8. Why is it so difficult for us to give up our rights?

_____

_____

_____

9. List some of the benefits of self-sacrifice.

_____

_____

_____

PRAYER

Father, long before we repented or even acknowledged our need for you, you sent your only Son to die for our sins. What amazing love! O Father, help us to be more like you. Fill us with your love, so that we will gladly sacrifice everything to win more souls for you. Take our eyes off ourselves, our rights, and desires. May we extend your hand of grace and mercy to the lost.

JOURNALING

Take a few moments to record your personal insights from this lesson.

What am I willing to give up to win more people to Christ?

ADDITIONAL QUESTIONS

10. Explain how a spirit of humility contributes to effective witnessing.

_____

_____

_____

11. How can we combat our natural tendency to fight for our rights?

_____

_____

_____

12. List some ways you can cultivate a spirit of humility.

_____

_____

_____

For more Bible passages on self-sacrifice, see Romans 12:1,2; Philippians 2:3–5; Hebrews 13:16; 1 Peter 2:5.

To complete the book of 1 Corinthians during this twelve–part study, read 1 Corinthians 7:1–9:27.

ADDITIONAL THOUGHTS

LESSON SIX

TEMPTATION

REFLECTION

Begin your study by sharing thoughts on this question.

1. Think of a time when you felt tempted by something. How did God help you?

_____

_____

_____

BIBLE READING

Read 1 Corinthians 10:1–13 from the NCV or the NKJV.

NCV

¹Brothers and sisters, I want you to know what happened to our ancestors who followed Moses. They were all under the cloud and all went through the sea. ²They were all baptized as followers of Moses in the cloud and in the sea. ³They all ate the same spiritual food, ⁴and all drank the same spiritual drink. They drank from that spiritual rock that followed them, and that rock was Christ. ⁵But God was not pleased with most of them, so they died in the desert.

⁶And these things happened as examples

NKJV

¹Moreover, brethren, I do not want you to be unaware that all our fathers were under the cloud, all passed through the sea, ²all were baptized into Moses in the cloud and in the sea, ³all ate the same spiritual food, ⁴and all drank the same spiritual drink. For they drank of that spiritual Rock that followed them, and that Rock was Christ. ⁵But with most of them God was not well pleased, for *their bodies* were scattered in the wilderness.

⁶Now these things became our examples, to the intent that we should not lust after evil

NCV

for us, to stop us from wanting evil things as those people did. [7]Do not worship idols, as some of them did. Just as it is written in the Scriptures: "They sat down to eat and drink, and then they got up and sinned sexually." [8]We must not take part in sexual sins, as some of them did. In one day twenty-three thousand of them died because of their sins. [9]We must not test Christ as some of them did; they were killed by snakes. [10]Do not complain as some of them did; they were killed by the angel that destroys.

[11]The things that happened to those people are examples. They were written down to teach us, because we live in a time when all these things of the past have reached their goal. [12]If you think you are strong, you should be careful not to fall. [13]The only temptation that has come to you is that which everyone has. But you can trust God, who will not permit you to be tempted more than you can stand. But when you are tempted, he will also give you a way to escape so that you will be able to stand it.

NKJV

things as they also lusted. [7]And do not become idolaters as *were* some of them. As it is written, "The people sat down to eat and drink, and rose up to play." [8]Nor let us commit sexual immorality, as some of them did, and in one day twenty-three thousand fell; [9]nor let us tempt Christ, as some of them also tempted, and were destroyed by serpents; [10]nor complain, as some of them also complained, and were destroyed by the destroyer. [11]Now all these things happened to them as examples, and they were written for our admonition, upon whom the ends of the ages have come.

[12]Therefore let him who thinks he stands take heed lest he fall. [13]No temptation has overtaken you except such as is common to man; but God *is* faithful, who will not allow you to be tempted beyond what you are able, but with the temptation will also make the way of escape, that you may be able to bear *it*.

DISCOVERY

Explore the Bible reading by discussing these questions.

2. How is Israel's history relevant to us today?

_____

_____

_____

3. What are some consequences of giving in to temptation over and over again?

_____

_____

_____

4. What does this passage reveal about the difference between human nature and God's character?

_____

_____

_____

5. What encouragement does Scripture offer us about facing temptation?

_____

_____

_____

6. List some of the ways God helps us resist sin.

_____

_____

_____

INSPIRATION

Here is an uplifting thought from *The Inspirational Bible*.

Real change is an inside job. You might alter things a day or two with money and systems, but the heart of the matter is, and always will be, the matter of the heart.

Allow me to get specific. Our problem is sin. Not finances. Not budgets. Not overcrowded prisons or drug dealers. Our problem is sin. We are in rebellion against our Creator. We are separated from our Father. We are cut off from the source of life. A new president or policy won't fix that. It can only be solved by God.

That's why the Bible uses drastic terms like *conversion*, *repentance*, and *lost* and *found*. Society may renovate, but only God re-creates.

Here is a practical exercise to put this truth into practice. The next time alarms go off in your world, ask yourself three questions.

1. Is there any unconfessed sin in my life? . . .
2. Are there any unresolved conflicts in my world? . . .
3. Are there any unsurrendered worries in my heart? . . .

Alarms serve a purpose. They signal a problem. Sometimes the problem is out there. More often it's in here. So before you peek outside, take a good look inside.

(From *When God Whispers Your Name* by Max Lucado)

RESPONSE

Use these questions to share more deeply with each other.

7. List some of the warning signs God uses to help us say no to sin.

_____

_____

_____

8. Why do we sometimes ignore the warning signs God provides?

_____

_____

_____

9. Think about a time when you gave in to temptation. What might have helped you be stronger?

_____

_____

_____

PRAYER

Father, your Word says that no temptation will be too strong for us to bear and that you will always show us a way to resist sin. We claim your promises and ask you to give us the strength to use the escape routes you provide. And we pray that in our hours of desperation and weakness, you would help us feel your presence.

JOURNALING

Take a few moments to record your personal insights from this lesson.

What keeps me from taking the escape routes that God provides?

ADDITIONAL QUESTIONS

10. Why is it important for us to understand our inclination toward sin?

_____

_____

_____

11. How does consistent time in God's Word fortify us in our areas of weakness?

_____

_____

_____

12. What do you plan to do differently the next time you are tempted?

_____

_____

_____

For more Bible passages on temptation, see Matthew 4:1–11; 26:41; Luke 11:4; Galatians 6:1; 1 Thessalonians 3:5; 1 Timothy 6:9; Hebrews 2:17,18; 4:15,16; James 1:13–15.

To complete the book of 1 Corinthians during this twelve–part study, read 1 Corinthians 10:1–13.

ADDITIONAL THOUGHTS

LESSON SEVEN

LIBERTY AND LOVE

REFLECTION

Begin your study by sharing thoughts on this question.

1. What new freedoms have you enjoyed since you became a Christian?

_____

_____

_____

BIBLE READING

Read 1 Corinthians 10:23–33 from the NCV or the NKJV.

NCV

23"We are allowed to do all things," but all things are not good for us to do. "We are allowed to do all things," but not all things help others grow stronger. 24Do not look out only for yourselves. Look out for the good of others also.

25Eat any meat that is sold in the meat market. Do not ask questions to see if it is meat you think is wrong to eat. 26You may eat it, "because the earth belongs to the Lord, and everything in it."

27Those who are not believers may invite you to eat with them. If you want to go, eat

NKJV

23All things are lawful for me, but not all things are helpful; all things are lawful for me, but not all things edify. 24Let no one seek his own, but each one the other's *well-being*.

25Eat whatever is sold in the meat market, asking no questions for conscience' sake; 26for "the earth *is* the LORD's, and all its fullness."

27If any of those who do not believe invites you *to dinner,* and you desire to go, eat whatever is set before you, asking no question for conscience' sake. 28But if anyone says to you, "This was offered to idols," do not eat it for the

NCV	NKJV

anything that is put before you. Do not ask questions to see if you think it might be wrong to eat. [28]But if anyone says to you, "That food was offered to idols," do not eat it. Do not eat it because of that person who told you and because eating it might be thought to be wrong. [29]I don't mean you think it is wrong, but the other person might. But why, you ask, should my freedom be judged by someone else's conscience? [30]If I eat the meal with thankfulness, why am I criticized because of something for which I thank God?

[31]The answer is, if you eat or drink, or if you do anything, do it all for the glory of God. [32]Never do anything that might hurt others—Jews, Greeks, or God's church—[33]just as I, also, try to please everybody in every way. I am not trying to do what is good for me but what is good for most people so they can be saved.

sake of the one who told you, and for conscience' sake; for "the earth is the LORD's, and all its fullness." [29]"Conscience," I say, not your own, but that of the other. For why is my liberty judged by another man's conscience? [30]But if I partake with thanks, why am I evil spoken of for the food over which I give thanks?

[31]Therefore, whether you eat or drink, or whatever you do, do all to the glory of God. [32]Give no offense, either to the Jews or to the Greeks or to the church of God, [33]just as I also please all men in all things, not seeking my own profit, but the profit of many, that they may be saved.

DISCOVERY

Explore the Bible reading by discussing these questions.

2. What limits our Christian freedom?

_____

_____

_____

3. Explain the relationship between our freedom to enjoy all of life and our limitations out of love for our sisters and brothers in Christ.

_____

_____

_____

4. What should Christians consider when making ethical decisions?

_____

_____

_____

5. What is meant by causing our weaker brothers and sisters to stumble in their faith?

_____

_____

_____

6. What should be our primary concern in making life-style choices?

_____

_____

_____

INSPIRATION

Here is an uplifting thought from *The Inspirational Bible*.

Loving others requires us to express our liberty wisely. In other words, love must rule. I'm not my own, I'm bought with a price. My goal is not to please me, it is to please my Lord Jesus, my God. It is not to please you, it is to please my Lord. The same is true for you. So the bottom line is this: I don't adapt my life according to what you may say, I adapt my life according to the basis of my love for you because I answer to Christ. And so do you.

. . . Even if you personally would not do what another is doing, let it be. And you who feel the freedom to do so, don't flaunt it or mock those who disagree. We are in the construction business, not destruction. And let's all remember that God's big-picture kingdom plan is not being shaped by small things like what one person prefers over another, but by large things, like righteousness and peace and joy.

(From *Grace Awakening*
by Charles Swindoll)

RESPONSE

Use these questions to share more deeply with each other.

7. What does it mean to express our liberty wisely?

_____

_____

_____

8. Explain the difference between tolerating differences and condoning wrong behavior.

_____

_____

_____

9. Why is it crucial for believers to love and accept one another?

_____

_____

_____

PRAYER

Father, help us realize that you have truly set us free—free from the lures of status and materialism and peer pressure. Remind us that when the Son sets us free, we are free indeed. And Father, show us when to sacrifice our rights out of love for each other. Fill us with your Spirit, so that our actions build up the church and bring glory to your name.

JOURNALING

Take a few moments to record your personal insights from this lesson.

In what ways can I find the balance between enjoying my freedom in Christ and giving up my rights to help others?

ADDITIONAL QUESTIONS

10. What characteristics of the world would be different if all Christians lived according to the guidelines in this lesson's Bible passage?

11. How can arguments over controversial issues harm the church?

12. Think of one person to whom you can show greater sensitivity and love. List some examples of how you can do that.

For more Bible passages on Christian freedom, see John 8:31–36; Romans 8:2; Galatians 4:4,5; 5:1–15; 1 Peter 2:16.

To complete the book of 1 Corinthians during this twelve–part study, read 1 Corinthians 10:14–11:34.

ADDITIONAL THOUGHTS

LESSON EIGHT

SPIRITUAL GIFTS

REFLECTION

Begin your study by sharing thoughts on this question.

1. Think of a role or responsibility you enjoy fulfilling in the church. Why do you enjoy it?

BIBLE READING

Read 1 Corinthians 12:1–11 from the NCV or the NKJV.

NCV

¹Now, brothers and sisters, I want you to understand about spiritual gifts. ²You know the way you lived before you were believers. You let yourselves be influenced and led away to worship idols—things that could not speak. ³So I want you to understand that no one who is speaking with the help of God's Spirit says, "Jesus be cursed." And no one can say, "Jesus is Lord," without the help of the Holy Spirit.

⁴There are different kinds of gifts, but they are all from the same Spirit. ⁵There are differ-

NKJV

¹Now concerning spiritual *gifts,* brethren, I do not want you to be ignorant: ²You know that you were Gentiles, carried away to these dumb idols, however you were led. ³Therefore I make known to you that no one speaking by the Spirit of God calls Jesus accursed, and no one can say that Jesus is Lord except by the Holy Spirit.

⁴There are diversities of gifts, but the same Spirit. ⁵There are differences of ministries, but the same Lord. ⁶And there are diversities of

NCV

ent ways to serve but the same Lord to serve. [6]And there are different ways that God works through people but the same God. God works in all of us in everything we do. [7]Something from the Spirit can be seen in each person, for the common good. [8]The Spirit gives one person the ability to speak with wisdom, and the same Spirit gives another the ability to speak with knowledge. [9]The same Spirit gives faith to one person. And, to another, that one Spirit gives gifts of healing. [10]The Spirit gives to another person the power to do miracles, to another the ability to prophesy. And he gives to another the ability to know the difference between good and evil spirits. The Spirit gives one person the ability to speak in different kinds of languages and to another the ability to interpret those languages. [11]One Spirit, the same Spirit, does all these things, and the Spirit decides what to give each person.

NKJV

activities, but it is the same God who works all in all. [7]But the manifestation of the Spirit is given to each one for the profit *of all:* [8]for to one is given the word of wisdom through the Spirit, to another the word of knowledge through the same Spirit, [9]to another faith by the same Spirit, to another gifts of healings by the same Spirit, [10]to another the working of miracles, to another prophecy, to another discerning of spirits, to another *different* kinds of tongues, to another the interpretation of tongues. [11]But one and the same Spirit works all these things, distributing to each one individually as He wills.

DISCOVERY

Explore the Bible reading by discussing these questions.

2. The Holy Spirit distributes spiritual gifts to all believers. Why is there such a variety of gifts?

_____

_____

_____

3. What is the purpose of our spiritual gifts?

_____

_____

_____

4. Though there are different gifts, there is only one God. Why is that important for us to remember?

_____

_____

_____

5. What is our responsibility in regard to our spiritual gifts?

_____

_____

_____

6. This passages says the Spirit gives a gift to everyone. Then why are there people who feel they have nothing to offer to their church?

_____

_____

_____

INSPIRATION

Here is an uplifting thought from *The Inspirational Bible.*

A few nights ago a peculiar thing happened.

An electrical storm caused a blackout in our neighborhood. When the lights went out, I felt my way through the darkness into the storage closet where we keep the candles for nights like this. . . . I took my match and lit four of them. . . .

I was turning to leave with the large candle in my hand when I heard a voice, "Now, hold it right there."

"Who said that?"

"I did." The voice was near my hand.

"Who are you? What are you?"

"I'm a candle."

I lifted up the candle to take a closer look. You won't believe what I saw. There was a tiny face in the wax . . . a moving, functioning, fleshlike face full of expression and life.

"Don't take me out of here!"

"What?"

"I said, Don't take me out of this room."

"What do you mean? I have to take you out. You're a candle. Your job is to give light. It's dark out there."

"But you can't take me out. I'm not ready," the candle explained with pleading eyes. "I need more preparation."

I couldn't believe my ears. "More preparation?"

"Yeah, I've decided I need to research this job of light-giving so I won't go out and make a bunch of mistakes. You'd be surprised how distorted the glow of an untrained candle can be. . . ."

"All right then," I said. "You're not the only candle on the shelf. I'll blow you out and take the others!"

But just as I got my cheeks full of air, I heard other voices.

"We aren't going either!"

. . . I turned around and looked at the three other candles. . . . "You are candles and your job is to light dark places!"

"Well, that may be what you think," said the candle on the far left. . . . "You may think we have to go, but I'm busy. . . . I'm meditating on the importance of light. It's really enlightening." . . .

"And you other two," I asked, "are you going to stay in here as well?"

A short, fat, purple candle with plump cheeks that reminded me of Santa Claus spoke up. "I'm waiting to get my life together. I'm not stable enough."

The last candle had a female voice, very pleasant to the ear. "I'd like to help," she explained, "but lighting the darkness is not my gift. . . . I'm a singer. I sing to other candles to encourage them to burn more brightly."

. . . She began a rendition of "This Little Light of Mine." . . . The other three joined in, filling the storage room with singing. . . . I took a step back and considered the absurdity of it all. Four perfectly healthy candles singing to each other about light but refusing to come out of the closet.

(From *God Came Near* by Max Lucado)

RESPONSE

Use these questions to share more deeply with each other.

7. What prevents us from using our gifts?

_____

_____

_____

8. In what ways can we help one another identify our spiritual gifts?

_____

_____

_____

9. What is one thing you could do this week to share your gifts?

_____

_____

_____

PRAYER

God, we want only to please you. But fear and anxiety keep us from serving you well. Father, give us the confidence to recognize our spiritual gifts and the courage to use them for your glory. Thank you for the assurance that our imperfect service cannot stand in the way of your amazing power. We give you all the glory for what you accomplish through us.

JOURNALING

Take a few moments to record your personal insights from this lesson.

In what ways have I personally benefited from the spiritual gifts of others?

ADDITIONAL QUESTIONS

10. What is wrong with saying that some gifts are superior to others?

_____

_____

_____

11. How can we use our gifts in a way that draws attention away from ourselves and gives the glory to God?

_____

_____

_____

12. In what ways does this lesson's Bible passage challenge you to change the way you serve in the church?

_____

_____

_____

For more Bible passages on spiritual gifts, see Romans 12:3–8; 1 Corinthians 7:7; 14:1–40; Ephesians 4:11–16; Hebrews 2:4; 1 Peter 4:10,11.

To complete the book of 1 Corinthians during this twelve–part study, read 1 Corinthians 12:1–11.

ADDITIONAL THOUGHTS

LESSON NINE

THE BODY OF CHRIST

REFLECTION

Begin your study by sharing thoughts on this question.

1. Think of a time when you felt a deep sense of unity among a group of believers. What were the contributing factors to that unity at that time?

_____

_____

_____

BIBLE READING

Read 1 Corinthians 12:12–26 from the NCV or the NKJV.

NCV

¹²A person's body is only one thing, but it has many parts. Though there are many parts to a body, all those parts make only one body. Christ is like that also. ¹³Some of us are Jews, and some are Greeks. Some of us are slaves, and some are free. But we were all baptized into one body through one Spirit. And we were all made to share in the one Spirit.

¹⁴The human body has many parts. ¹⁵The foot might say, "Because I am not a hand, I am not part of the body." But saying this would not

NKJV

¹²For as the body is one and has many members, but all the members of that one body, being many, are one body, so also *is* Christ. ¹³For by one Spirit we were all baptized into one body—whether Jews or Greeks, whether slaves or free—and have all been made to drink into one Spirit. ¹⁴For in fact the body is not one member but many.

¹⁵If the foot should say, "Because I am not a hand, I am not of the body," is it therefore not of the body? ¹⁶And if the ear should say, "Be-

NCV

stop the foot from being a part of the body. [16]The ear might say, "Because I am not an eye, I am not part of the body." But saying this would not stop the ear from being a part of the body. [17]If the whole body were an eye, it would not be able to hear. If the whole body were an ear, it would not be able to smell. [18-19]If each part of the body were the same part, there would be no body. But truly God put all the parts, each one of them, in the body as he wanted them. [20]So then there are many parts, but only one body.

[21]The eye cannot say to the hand, "I don't need you!" And the head cannot say to the foot, "I don't need you!" [22]No! Those parts of the body that seem to be the weaker are really necessary. [23]And the parts of the body we think are less deserving are the parts to which we give the most honor. We give special respect to the parts we want to hide. [24]The more respectable parts of our body need no special care. But God put the body together and gave more honor to the parts that need it [25]so our body would not be divided. God wanted the different parts to care the same for each other. [26]If one part of the body suffers, all the other parts suffer with it. Or if one part of our body is honored, all the other parts share its honor.

NKJV

cause I am not an eye, I am not of the body," is it therefore not of the body? [17]If the whole body *were* an eye, where *would be* the hearing? If the whole *were* hearing, where *would be* the smelling? [18]But now God has set the members, each one of them, in the body just as He pleased. [19]And if they *were* all one member, where *would* the body *be?*

[20]But now indeed *there are* many members, yet one body. [21]And the eye cannot say to the hand, "I have no need of you"; nor again the head to the feet, "I have no need of you." [22]No, much rather, those members of the body which seem to be weaker are necessary. [23]And those *members* of the body which we think to be less honorable, on these we bestow greater honor; and our unpresentable *parts* have greater modesty, [24]but our presentable *parts* have no need. But God composed the body, having given greater honor to that *part* which lacks it, [25]that there should be no schism in the body, but *that* the members should have the same care for one another. [26]And if one member suffers, all the members suffer with *it;* or if one member is honored, all the members rejoice with *it.*

DISCOVERY

Explore the Bible reading by discussing these questions.

2. This passage compares the body of Christ to a human body. How would you compare them in your own words?

_____

_____

_____

3. In what ways are the various members of the church dependent on each other?

_____

_____

_____

4. This scripture warns against any part of the body considering itself either less important or more important than the others. This is a warning to us about what kind of parallel behavior in the church?

_____

_____

_____

5. Why did God give more honor to certain parts of the body of Christ?

_____

_____

_____

6. We are to honor each other as other parts of the same body. In light of that, how does God want us to treat each other?

_____

_____

_____

INSPIRATION

Here is an uplifting thought from *The Inspirational Bible*.

There was some dice-throwing that went on at the foot of the cross. . . . I've wondered what that scene must have looked like to Jesus. As he looked downward past his bloody feet at the circle of gamblers, what did he think? What emotions did he feel? He must have been amazed. Here are common soldiers witnessing the world's most uncommon event and they don't know it. As far as they're concerned, it's just another Friday morning and he is just another criminal. "Come on. hurry up; it's my turn!"

"All right, all right—this throw is for the sandals."

Casting lots for the possessions of Christ. Heads ducked. Eyes downward. Cross forgotten.

The symbolism is striking. Do you see it?

It makes me think of us. The religious. Those who claim heritage at the cross. I'm thinking of all of us. Every believer in the land. The stuffy. The loose. The strict. The simple. Upper church. Lower church. "Spirit-filled."

Millenialists. Evangelical. Political. Mystical. Literal. Cynical. Robes. Collars. Three-piece suits. Born-againers. Ameners.

I'm thinking of us.

I'm thinking that we aren't so unlike those soldiers. (I'm sorry to say.)

We, too, play games at the foot of the cross. We compete for members. We scramble for status. We deal our judgments and condemnations. Competition. Selfishness. Personal gain. It's all there. We don't like what the other did so we take the sandal we won and walk away in a huff.

So close to the timbers yet so far from the blood.

We are so close to the world's most uncommon event, but we act like common crapshooters huddled in bickering groups and fighting over silly opinions.

How many pulpit hours have been wasted on preaching the trivial? How many churches have tumbled at the throes of miniscuity? How many leaders have saddled their pet peeves, drawn their swords of bitterness and launched into battle against brethren over issues that are not worth discussing?

So close to the cross but so far from the Christ.

We specialize in "I am right" rallies. We write books about what the other does wrong. We major in finding gossip and become experts in unveiling weaknesses. We split into little huddles and then, God forbid, we split again. . . .

Are our differences that divisive? Are our opinions that obtrusive? Are our walls that wide? Is it *that* impossible to find a common cause?

"May they all be one," Jesus prayed.

One. Not one in groups of two thousand. But one in One. *One* church. *One* faith. *One* Lord. Not Baptist, not Methodist, not Adventist. Just Christian. No denominations. No hierarchies. No traditions. Just Christ.

Too idealistic? Impossible to achieve? I don't think so. Harder things have been done, you know. For example, once upon a tree, a Creator gave his life for his creation. Maybe all we need are a few hearts that are willing to follow suit.

(From *No Wonder They Call Him the Savior* by Max Lucado)

RESPONSE

Use these questions to share more deeply with each other.

7. Why should we resist the temptation to compete with or compare ourselves to other believers?

_____

_____

_____

8. In what ways do petty arguments and divisions in the church tarnish the gospel message?

_____

_____

_____

9. How can we learn to appreciate each other's differences, instead of allowing them to divide us?

_____

_____

_____

PRAYER

Father, we know that disputes and divisions don't belong in the body of Christ. But sometimes we hold on to our hurts waiting for others to take the first step toward reconciliation. Give us courage, Father, to swallow our pride and reach out in love to our Christian brothers and sisters. Help us to look past our differences and focus on the common ground we share in you.

JOURNALING

Take a few moments to record your personal insights from this lesson.

Since I'm an important member of the body of Christ, what can I do to help the body of Christ function most effectively?

ADDITIONAL QUESTIONS

10. What threatens the unity of your local church?

_____

_____

_____

11. What steps can you take to promote peace and harmony in your church?

_____

_____

_____

12. In what ways can you honor someone in your church who may feel unappreciated or insignificant?

_____

_____

_____

For more Bible passages on the body of Christ, see Romans 12:4–6; 1 Corinthians 14:4–26; Ephesians 4:25; 5:23–32; Colossians 1:18, 24,25.

To complete the book of 1 Corinthians during this twelve–part study, read 1 Corinthians 12:12–31.

LESSON TEN

TRUE LOVE

REFLECTION

Begin your study by sharing thoughts on this question.

1. How does it feel to receive an extravagant present from someone you love?

_____

_____

_____

BIBLE READING

Read 1 Corinthians 13:1–13 from the NCV or the NKJV.

NCV

¹I may speak in different languages of people or even angels. But if I do not have love, I am only a noisy bell or a crashing cymbal. ²I may have the gift of prophecy. I may understand all the secret things of God and have all knowledge, and I may have faith so great I can move mountains. But even with all these things, if I do not have love, then I am nothing. ³I may give away everything I have, and I may even give my body as an offering to be burned. But I gain nothing if I do not have love.

NKJV

¹Though I speak with the tongues of men and of angels, but have not love, I have become sounding brass or a clanging cymbal. ²And though I have *the gift of* prophecy, and understand all mysteries and all knowledge, and though I have all faith, so that I could remove mountains, but have not love, I am nothing. ³And though I bestow all my goods to feed *the poor,* and though I give my body to be burned, but have not love, it profits me nothing.

⁴Love suffers long *and* is kind; love does not envy; love does not parade itself, is not puffed

NCV

[4]Love is patient and kind. Love is not jealous, it does not brag, and it is not proud. [5]Love is not rude, is not selfish, and does not get upset with others. Love does not count up wrongs that have been done. [6]Love is not happy with evil but is happy with the truth. [7]Love patiently accepts all things. It always trusts, always hopes, and always remains strong.

[8]Love never ends. There are gifts of prophecy, but they will be ended. There are gifts of speaking in different languages, but those gifts will stop. There is the gift of knowledge, but it will come to an end. [9]The reason is that our knowledge and our ability to prophesy are not perfect. [10]But when perfection comes, the things that are not perfect will end. [11]When I was a child, I talked like a child, I thought like a child, I reasoned like a child. When I became a man, I stopped those childish ways. [12]It is the same with us. Now we see a dim reflection, as if we were looking into a mirror, but then we shall see clearly. Now I know only a part, but then I will know fully, as God has known me. [13]So these three things continue forever: faith, hope, and love. And the greatest of these is love.

NKJV

up; [5]does not behave rudely, does not seek its own, is not provoked, thinks no evil; [6]does not rejoice in iniquity, but rejoices in the truth; [7]bears all things, believes all things, hopes all things, endures all things.

[8]Love never fails. But whether *there are* prophecies, they will fail; whether *there are* tongues, they will cease; whether *there is* knowledge, it will vanish away. [9]For we know in part and we prophesy in part. [10]But when that which is perfect has come, then that which is in part will be done away.

[11]When I was a child, I spoke as a child, I understood as a child, I thought as a child; but when I became a man, I put away childish things. [12]For now we see in a mirror, dimly, but then face to face. Now I know in part, but then I shall know just as I also am known.

[13]And now abide faith, hope, love, these three; but the greatest of these *is* love.

DISCOVERY

Explore the Bible reading by discussing these questions.

2. Even the best gifts are worthless if they aren't given in love. Why?

_____

_____

_____

3. How can spiritual gifts be wasted?

_____

_____

_____

4. This passage describes love with words like patient, kind, accepting, trusting. What can you add to that list?

_____

_____

_____

5. What does true love require of us?

_____

_____

_____

6. The love described in this passage is selfless and always faithful. Why is it difficult to demonstrate that kind of love?

_____

_____

_____

INSPIRATION

Here is an uplifting thought from *The Inspirational Bible*.

As the husband looks in the jewelry case, he rationalizes, "Sure she would want the watch, but it's too expensive. She's a practical woman, she'll understand. I'll just get the bracelet today. I'll buy the watch . . . someday."

Someday. The enemy of risky love is a snake whose tongue has mastered the talk of deception. "Someday," he hisses.

"Someday, I can take her on the cruise."

"Someday, I will have time to call and chat."

"Someday, the children will understand why I was so busy."

But you know the truth, don't you? You know even before I write it. You could say it better than I.

Somedays never come.

And the price of practicality is sometimes higher than extravagance.

But the rewards of risky love are always greater than its cost.

Go to the effort. Invest the time. Write the letter. Make the apology. Take the trip. Purchase the gift. Do it. The seized opportunity renders joy. The neglected brings regret.

(From *And the Angels Were Silent* by Max Lucado)

RESPONSE

Use these questions to share more deeply with each other.

7. What sometimes keeps us from showing our love for others?

_____

_____

_____

8. What can we learn from Christ's example about loving extravagantly and without limits?

_____

_____

_____

9. In what ways can God's love free us to love others?

_____

_____

_____

PRAYER

Father, the fact that you became flesh and dwelt among us proves that you love us far beyond our worth. We ask you, Father, to fill us to overflowing with your love, so that it flows freely from us to others. Let our lives be testimonies of your love so that when people look at us they see a glimpse of your deep love for them.

JOURNALING

Take a few moments to record your personal insights from this lesson.

What are some ways I have felt God's love for me?

ADDITIONAL QUESTIONS

10. Explain unconditional love.

_____

_____

_____

11. When have you seen God's love transform a person?

_____

_____

_____

12. In what ways can you extend God's love to someone today?

_____

_____

_____

For more Bible passages on love, see Matthew 5:43–46; Luke 6:35; John 13:34,35; Romans 5:5–8; Galatians 5:14; Ephesians 3:16–19; Hebrews 10:24; 1 Peter 1:22; 1 John 3:11–23.

To complete the book of 1 Corinthians during this twelve–part study, read 1 Corinthians 13:1–14:40.

ADDITIONAL THOUGHTS

LESSON ELEVEN

CHRIST'S VICTORY OVER DEATH

REFLECTION

Begin your study by sharing thoughts on this question.

1. Think about what your friends believe about life after death. How do your beliefs differ?

_____

_____

_____

BIBLE READING

Read 1 Corinthians 15:20–34 from the NCV or the NKJV.

NCV

²⁰But Christ has truly been raised from the dead—the first one and proof that those who sleep in death will also be raised. ²¹Death has come because of what one man did, but the rising from death also comes because of one man. ²²In Adam all of us die. In the same way, in Christ all of us will be made alive again. ²³But everyone will be raised to life in the right order. Christ was first to be raised. When Christ comes again, those who belong to him will be raised to life, ²⁴and then the end will come. At

NKJV

²⁰But now Christ is risen from the dead, *and* has become the firstfruits of those who have fallen asleep. ²¹For since by man *came* death, by Man also *came* the resurrection of the dead. ²²For as in Adam all die, even so in Christ all shall be made alive. ²³But each one in his own order: Christ the firstfruits, afterward those *who are* Christ's at His coming. ²⁴Then *comes* the end, when He delivers the kingdom to God the Father, when He puts an end to all rule and all authority and power. ²⁵For He must reign till

that time Christ will destroy all rulers, authorities, and powers, and he will hand over the kingdom to God the Father. ²⁵Christ must rule until he puts all enemies under his control. ²⁶The last enemy to be destroyed will be death. ²⁷The Scripture says that God put all things under his control. When it says "all things" are under him, it is clear this does not include God himself. God is the One who put everything under his control. ²⁸After everything has been put under the Son, then he will put himself under God, who had put all things under him. Then God will be the complete ruler over everything.

²⁹If the dead are never raised, what will people do who are being baptized for the dead? If the dead are not raised at all, why are people being baptized for them?

³⁰And what about us? Why do we put ourselves in danger every hour? ³¹I die every day. That is true, brothers and sisters, just as it is true that I brag about you in Christ Jesus our Lord. ³²If I fought wild animals in Ephesus only with human hopes, I have gained nothing. If the dead are not raised, "Let us eat and drink, because tomorrow we will die."

³³Do not be fooled: "Bad friends will ruin good habits." ³⁴Come back to your right way of thinking and stop sinning. Some of you do not know God—I say this to shame you.

He has put all enemies under His feet. ²⁶The last enemy *that* will be destroyed *is* death. ²⁷For "He has put all things under His feet." But when He says "all things are put under *Him*," *it is* evident that He who put all things under Him is excepted. ²⁸Now when all things are made subject to Him, then the Son Himself will also be subject to Him who put all things under Him, that God may be all in all.

²⁹Otherwise, what will they do who are baptized for the dead, if the dead do not rise at all? Why then are they baptized for the dead? ³⁰And why do we stand in jeopardy every hour? ³¹I affirm, by the boasting in you which I have in Christ Jesus our Lord, I die daily. ³²If, in the manner of men, I have fought with beasts at Ephesus, what advantage *is it* to me? If *the* dead do not rise, "Let us eat and drink, for tomorrow we die!"

³³Do not be deceived: "Evil company corrupts good habits." ³⁴Awake to righteousness, and do not sin; for some do not have the knowledge of God. I speak *this* to your shame.

DISCOVERY

Explore the Bible reading by discussing these questions.

2. This passage draws a comparison between Adam's death and Christ's death. What did the death of Christ give us that Adam's death didn't?

_____

_____

_____

3. What proof do you see that there is life after death?

_____

_____

_____

4. Sin entered the world when man sinned against God. How will Christ's death eventually destroy sin?

_____

_____

_____

5. Believing there is life after death helped Paul face danger and endure hardship. How does that same belief help us face life?

_____

_____

_____

6. What hope does Christ's resurrection offer?

_____

_____

_____

INSPIRATION

Here is an uplifting thought from *The Inspirational Bible*.

A sudden breeze, surprisingly warm, whistles through the leaves scattering dust from the lifeless form. And with the breath of fresh air comes the difference. Winging on the warm wind is his image. Laughter is laid in the sculpted cheeks. A reservoir of tears is stored in the soul. A sprinkling of twinkle for the eyes. Poetry for the spirit. Logic. Loyalty. Like leaves on an autumn breeze, they float and land and are absorbed. His gifts become a part of him.

His Majesty smiles at his image. "It is good."

The eyes open.

Oneness. Creator and created walking on the river bank. Laughter. Purity. Innocent joy. Life unending.

Then the tree.

The struggle. The snake. The lie. The enticement. Heart torn, lured. Soul drawn to pleasure, to independence, to importance. Inner agony. Whose will?

The choice. Death of innocence. Entrance of death. The fall.

Tearstains mingling with fruit-stains. . . .

[Then,] The Quest.

"Abram, you will father a nation! And Abram—tell the people I love them."

"Moses, you will deliver my people! And Moses—tell the people I love them."

"Joshua, you will lead the chosen ones! And Joshua—tell the people I love them."

"David, you will reign over the people! And David—tell the people I love them."

"Jeremiah, you will bear tidings of bondage! But Jeremiah, remind my children, remind my children that I love them."

Altars. Sacrifices. Rebelling. Returning. Reacting. Repenting. Romance. Tablets. Judges. Pillars. Bloodshed. Wars. Kings. Giants. Law. Hezekiah. Nehemiah. Hosea. . . . God watching, never turning, ever loving, ever yearning for the Garden again. . . .

[Finally,] Empty throne. Spirit descending. Hushed angels.

A girl . . . a womb . . . an egg.

The same Divine Artist again forms a body. This time his own. Fleshly divinity. Skin layered on spirit. Omnipotence with hair. Toenails. Knuckles. Molars. Kneecaps. Once again he walks with man. Yet the Garden is now thorny. Thorns that cut, thorns that poison, thorns that remain lodged, leaving bitter wounds. Disharmony. Sickness. Betrayal. Fear. Guilt.

The lions no longer pause. The clouds no longer hover. The birds scatter too quickly. Disharmony. Competition. Blindness.

And once again, a tree.

Once again the struggle. The snake. The enticement. Heart torn, lured. Once again the question, "Whose will?"

Then the choice. Tearstains mingle with bloodstains. Relationship restored. Bridge erected.

Once again he smiles. "It is good."

"For just as death came by the means of a man, in the same way the rising from death comes by means of a man. For just as all people die because of their union with Adam, in the same way all will be raised to life because of their union with Christ" (1 Corinthians 15:21–22 TEV).

(From *God Came Near* by Max Lucado)

RESPONSE

Use these questions to share more deeply with each other.

7. What recurring theme is seen in the history of God's relationship with people?

_____

_____

_____

8. Why did God send his Son to earth to die?

_____

_____

_____

9. In what way is Christ's victory over death essential to our faith?

_____

_____

_____

PRAYER

We praise you, Jesus, for conquering death for us. Your resurrection gives us hope that we will one day rise with you. Until that day, help us to remain faithful. Give us a glimpse into the everlasting so we will live for you whatever the cost. May we see the joy that is before us, and may we set our hopes on spending eternity with you.

JOURNALING

Take a few moments to record your personal insights from this lesson.

How can I know for certain that I will be raised with Christ?

ADDITIONAL QUESTIONS

10. In what ways would your life be different if you did not believe in life after death?

_____

_____

_____

11. Describe what Christ's resurrection means to you.

_____

_____

_____

12. How should the truth of this lesson's Bible passage affect the way you live today?

_____

_____

_____

For more Bible passages on Christ's victory over death, see Isaiah 25:7,8; 53:10–12; John 5:24–29; Romans 4:25; 5:12–21; 2 Timothy 1:10; Hebrews 2:14–15.

To complete the book of 1 Corinthians during this twelve-part study, read 1 Corinthians 15:1–58.

LESSON TWELVE

GIVING TO GOD'S WORK

REFLECTION

Begin your study by sharing thoughts on this question.

1. Think of a time when you have found great joy in giving to a charity or a church. How was it a blessing to you?

_____

_____

_____

BIBLE READING

Read 1 Corinthians 16:1–11 from the NCV or the NKJV.

NCV

¹Now I will write about the collection of money for God's people. Do the same thing I told the Galatian churches to do: ²On the first day of every week, each one of you should put aside money as you have been blessed. Save it up so you will not have to collect money after I come. ³When I arrive, I will send whomever you approve to take your gift to Jerusalem. I will send them with letters of introduction, ⁴and if it seems good for me to go also, they will go along with me.

NKJV

¹Now concerning the collection for the saints, as I have given orders to the churches of Galatia, so you must do also: ²On the first *day* of the week let each one of you lay something aside, storing up as he may prosper, that there be no collections when I come. ³And when I come, whomever you approve by *your* letters I will send to bear your gift to Jerusalem. ⁴But if it is fitting that I go also, they will go with me.

⁵Now I will come to you when I pass through Macedonia (for I am passing through

NCV

⁵I plan to go through Macedonia, so I will come to you after I go through there. ⁶Perhaps I will stay with you for a time or even all winter. Then you can help me on my trip, wherever I go. ⁷I do not want to see you now just in passing. I hope to stay a longer time with you if the Lord allows it. ⁸But I will stay at Ephesus until Pentecost, ⁹because a good opportunity for a great and growing work has been given to me now. And there are many people working against me.

¹⁰If Timothy comes to you, see to it that he has nothing to fear with you, because he is working for the Lord just as I am. ¹¹So none of you should treat Timothy as unimportant, but help him on his trip in peace so that he can come back to me. I am expecting him to come with the brothers.

NKJV

Macedonia). ⁶And it may be that I will remain, or even spend the winter with you, that you may send me on my journey, wherever I go. ⁷For I do not wish to see you now on the way; but I hope to stay a while with you, if the Lord permits.

⁸But I will tarry in Ephesus until Pentecost. ⁹For a great and effective door has opened to me, and *there are* many adversaries.

¹⁰And if Timothy comes, see that he may be with you without fear; for he does the work of the Lord, as I also *do*. ¹¹Therefore let no one despise him. But send him on his journey in peace, that he may come to me; for I am waiting for him with the brethren.

DISCOVERY

Explore the Bible reading by discussing these questions.

2. Paul advised the Corinthian church to collect money to support other Christians. In what ways do we follow Paul's advice today?

_____

_____

_____

3. Paul instructed the Corinthians to save up their offering ahead of time rather than waiting until he came to start collecting. What was the advantage to this plan?

_____

_____

_____

4. In what ways are the guidelines in this passage applicable to believers today?

_____

_____

_____

5. What guidelines can we use to know how much money to give to the church?

_____

_____

_____

6. Timothy wasn't as prominent as Paul, yet Paul instructed the Corinthians to treat Timothy as an important person. Why?

_____

_____

_____

INSPIRATION

Here is an uplifting thought from *The Inspirational Bible*.

You don't give for God's sake. You give for your sake. "The purpose of tithing is to teach you to always put God first in your lives" (Deut. 14:23 TLB). In what ways does tithing teach you? Consider the simple act of writing a check for the offering. First you enter the date. Already you are reminded that you are a time-bound creature and every possession you have will rust or burn. Best to give it while you can.

Then you enter the name of the one to whom you are giving the money. If the bank would cash it, you'd write *God*. But they won't, so you write the name of the church or group that has earned your trust.

Next comes the amount. Ahh, the moment of truth. You're more than a person with a checkbook. You're David, placing a stone in the sling. You're Peter, one foot on the boat, one foot on the lake. You're a little boy in a big crowd. A picnic lunch is all the Teacher needs, but it's all you have.

What will you do? Sling the Stone? Take the Step? Give the Meal?

Careful now, don't move too quickly. You aren't just entering an amount . . . you are making a confession. A confession that God owns it all anyway.

And then the line in the lower left-hand corner on which you write what the check is for. Hard to know what to put. It's for the light bills and literature. A little bit of outreach. A little bit of salary.

Better yet, it's partial payment for what the church has done to help you raise your family . . . keep your own priorities sorted out . . . tune you in to his ever-nearness.

Or, perhaps, best yet, it's for you. It's a moment for you to clip yet another strand from the rope of earth so that when he returns you won't be tied up.

(From *When God Whispers Your Name* by Max Lucado)

RESPONSE

Use these questions to share more deeply with each other.

7. What are the purposes of tithing?

_____

_____

_____

8. Think of a lesson you have learned through giving your money to God's work. Why does giving often result in a learning experience?

_____

_____

_____

9. List some principles or "rules of the road" that help you be a good manager of God's money.

_____

_____

_____

PRAYER

Father, you've been so good to us. Everything we have comes from your gracious hand. Forgive us, Father, for clinging too tightly to the things you have given us. Teach us to give generously and sacrificially to your work. Help us to put you first, in every area of our lives.

JOURNALING

Take a few moments to record your personal insights from this lesson.

What does my checkbook reveal to me about my priorities?

ADDITIONAL QUESTIONS

10. Explain why financial stewardship is important.

_____

_____

_____

11. Why is it sometimes difficult to give generously to God's work?

_____

_____

_____

12. Think of an improvement you could make, in light of this lesson's Bible passage, in the way you manage your money. How would that improvement change the way you give?

_____

_____

_____

For more Bible passages on giving to God, see Genesis 28:22; Leviticus 27:30; Deuteronomy 15:10,11; Matthew 22:21; Acts 20:35; Romans 12:6–8; 2 Corinthians 9:7–15.

To complete the book of 1 Corinthians during this twelve–part study, read 1 Corinthians 16:1–24.

ADDITIONAL THOUGHTS

ADDITIONAL THOUGHTS

108

ADDITIONAL THOUGHTS

LEADERS' NOTES

LESSON ONE

Question 2: As you discuss what seems foolish about the gospel, ask group members about their initial encounter with the Gospel of Christ. What age were they? What was hard for them to accept? What were some misconceptions they may have had about following Christ?

Question 6: Bragging or boasting implies a certain amount of pride. Discuss the difference between the sin of being prideful and the wonderful pride that we have in Jesus' accomplishments. (The difference resides in whether the object of our pride is ourselves.) In contemplating what God has done for us, see Romans 5:8 and 2 Corinthians 5:21.

Question 7: Be sure to include music, printed materials, and billboard advertising when considering the media. What commercials use sex to sell something totally unrelated? How are conservatives depicted in the news? When do news stories or movies prompt us to sympathize with the less-than-honorable characters or choices?

Question 8: See Proverbs 3:5-7. For more discussion, how should we draw the balance between acting on the wisdom God gave us and trusting him to lead? Ask your group for any personal experiences.

LESSON TWO

Question 2: Scripture tells us often that we are not able to comprehend everything in reality as God knows it. Discuss the fact that there are some things we may consider "hidden" that are just not understandable to us now. Also point out that part of the necessity of faith is trusting God with those things that we do not, as of yet, understand.

Question 4: For more on the Holy Spirit see John 14:26; 15:26; 16:13-15; 1 John 2:27.

Question 5: Compare a tone-deaf person's appreciation for music and an unsaved person's understanding of the truths of God.

Question 6: We can never really know what God is thinking (Romans 11:34), but because we have the Holy Spirit, we can develop a relationship with God. And, as with any relationship, when you spend time with someone, you begin to understand his thoughts, plans, and ways. After years of marriage couples begin to finish each other's sentences and know each other's thoughts. It is the same with God. As you spend time with Christ in his word and prayer and your relationship develops, you begin to gain the mind of Christ.

Question 7: What are the many ways in our world that we gain wisdom? Discuss the different kinds of schooling. Discuss the difference between head knowledge and common sense. You may even ask if anyone has known an "absent-minded professor type" who had plenty of book knowledge, but not common sense.

LESSON THREE

Question 2: You may want to discuss the role of a foundation in a house. What does it do for the house? Keeps it stable, keeps it from sinking...

Question 4: If you have someone in construction in your group or someone who has recently had his house inspected, ask about the inspection process. What kinds of tests tell us the strength of building materials?

Question 6: If you like using visuals, you may want to take a small amount of straw and some bricks (or chips of bricks) to class. Place the bricks inside a fire-proof bowl and light them, or try to. Then burn up the straw.

Question 8: Follow with this question: What are some of the pitfalls of measuring our success by external results? Also, what are some other options for measuring success?

Question 9: After discussing what kind of work counts for eternity, brainstorm the everyday concerns that sometimes keep us from doing eternity work.

Question 12: You can take this question a step further by encouraging the group members to commit to one of the listed ways to invest in God's kingdom. Is there a way for the group to commit to making one of these investments together?

LESSON FOUR

Question 2: Here, the term "spiritual pride" refers to one Christian judging whether a fellow Christian is a good follower of Christ. Often that results in arrogance. Evaluating others tempts us with the attitude that we are better than they are. If your group doesn't include it in their answers, discuss the long-term effects of this kind of pride: church splits, discouraged believers, loss of witness, etc.

Question 5: After answering this question, compare Paul's attitude toward status and position with the attitude in your culture. What are the messages that your group receives from their places of work and even their church about status?

Question 9: It is important to examine the motives behind our service. Ask your group for personal examples of when they have had to do some soul-searching regarding their motives.

Question 10: Ask the group what feeds our appetite for prestige and power, while you discuss how we can curb that appetite.

Question 12: You may want to ask for examples of public figures who have openly given God the glory for their success. Discuss what holds us back from being open about our faith.

LESSON FIVE

Question 3: Paul was a servant to all people. He did what it took to find common ground with those he was with and made himself available to them in order to win them to Christ. For more on serving, see Galatians 5:13.

Question 6: Be prepared to share something that could be hindering your Christian witness.

Question 9: For more on the benefits of self sacrifice, see Matthew 19: 21 and Luke 14:16.

LESSON SIX

Question 3: See Numbers 14 for insight into the consequences of sinning again and again.

Question 7: Can your group think of any other warning signs they experience in life (and perhaps ignore from time to time). As the leader, you might share some personal warning signs God has used to help you say no to sin.

Question 10: You may want to brainstorm together the traits of a society that has no understanding of their inclination to sin.

LESSON SEVEN

Question 4: You may want to take the time to define what ethical decisions are, both between right and wrong and shades of gray.

Question 6: See also Romans 14.

Question 8: This could be a sensitive question as certain differences to some people are considered wrong behavior to others. Be careful not to get off on a tangent because of that. Let each person tell his or her own drawn lines, even if they are different from someone else's.

Question 9: It is important to remember that we are in the construction business, not in the destruction business. We are to be furthering God's kingdom, and that cannot be accomplished if we do not love and accept our fellow believers. See 1 John 4:7-8.

LESSON EIGHT

Question 4: Though there are different gifts, God is the source of them all, and they are to be used for his glory and the furthering of his kingdom. This enables us to be unified. Sure, we have different gifts and abilities, but our faith is wrapped around our God, not our gifts. For other Scriptures on gifts, see Romans 12:3-8 and Ephesians 4:1-13.

Question 6: Some members of your group may feel they have nothing to offer their church because they have not identified their spiritual gifts or because they aren't confident enough to use those gifts. Be prepared with ideas about some of the gifts represented in your group. Think about the ministries of your congregation and how those gifts could be used.

Question 7: Some group members may be timid about sharing, so be prepared to share first. In most cases some people don't use their gifts because someone else can "do it better." While we do want to serve God with excellence, what he really asks is our personal best, not our competitive best. You may want to discuss this with your group pointing out that most gifts require practice to increase skill in using them. If we don't practice our gifts because they aren't good enough, then they don't ever get any better.

Question 8: Take time as a group at the end of this lesson or on a separate occasion to help members identify their spiritual gifts.

LESSON NINE

Question 4: Be careful not to get into a gripe session. Keep the conversation moving toward how the church can be more unified.

Question 7: You may want to examine what happens when people do compete and compare themselves to each other. Read 2 Corinthians 10:12.

Question 8: This question can concern both a community wide reputation as well as individuals who come to the church. Discuss what a seeker or newcomer to the faith thinks when he sees petty arguments and divisions in the church.

LESSON TEN

Question 3: Be sensitive to the fact that you probably have some group members that can be very hard on themselves. While you are discussing wasting gifts, mention some hopeful thoughts like reclaiming the usefulness of our gifts, or that God's forgiveness allows us to start fresh even when we've wasted time or gifts.

Question 6: You may want to mention a recent experience from your own life where you found it difficult to maintain an attitude of love.

Question 8: Mention some examples of compassion from Christ's life, such as Matthew 9:35-36; Mark 8:1-5; John 11:32-35.

LESSON ELEVEN

Question 3: Historically our proof that there is life after death is in the eyewitnesses who touched and interacted with Jesus after he had been crucified and died on the cross. Let your group give their own subjective reasoning and insight as well.

Question 5: Discuss everyday ramifications of this question. What overall perspective on life does our belief in life after death give us that makes a difference in the annoyances of our everyday details.

Question 6: Christ's resurrection is the guarantee of our eventual resurrection to eternal life. For other scriptures, see Romans 6:5; Philippians 3:10; 1 Peter 1:3.

Question 8: Have group members look up and read aloud these Scriptures during the discussion: Romans 5:6-8; Hebrews 9:27-28; 1 Peter 2:23-25.

Question 9: See also Romans 4:25; 5:12-19.

LESSON TWELVE

Question 3: Discuss how this plan might help some of the church's financial needs represented within your group.

Question 5: For some verses from the Old Testament about tithing, see Leviticus 27:30; Numbers 18:28; 2 Chronicles 31:5-6; Nehemiah 10:35-38.

Question 6: Timothy was young, and it was possible that the Corinthians might look down on him or not listen to him because of his youth.

Question 8: Be prepared to share your answer first. Luke 6:28 might prompt some discussion on giving to God.

Question 10: Be sure to include reasons such as discipline, helping missionaries, and helping not only your own local church, but the whole church of Christ as well.

ADDITIONAL NOTES

ADDITIONAL NOTES

ADDITIONAL NOTES

ADDITIONAL NOTES

ADDITIONAL NOTES

ACKNOWLEDGMENTS

Keller, Philip. *A Gardener Looks at the Fruits of the Spirit*, copyright 1986, Word, Inc., Dallas, Texas.

Lucado, Max. *And the Angels Were Silent*, copyright 1992 by Max Lucado, Questar Publishers, Multnomah Books .

Lucado, Max. *God Came Near*, copyright 1987, Questar Publishers, Multnomah Books .

Lucado, Max. *In the Eye of the Storm,* copyright 1991, Word, Inc., Dallas, Texas.

Lucado, Max. *No Wonder They Call Him the Savior,* copyright 1986 by Max Lucado, Questar Publishers, Multnomah Books .

Lucado, Max. *When God Whispers Your Name,* copyright 1994, Word, Inc., Dallas, Texas.

Swindoll, Charles. *The Grace Awakening,* copyright 1990, Word, Inc., Dallas, Texas.

Swindoll, Charles. *Living on the Ragged Edge,* copyright 1985 Word, Inc., Dallas, Texas.

Yohn, Rick. *Finding Time*, copyright 1984, Thomas Nelson, Nashville, Tennessee.